flowers
at home

Dedication

To Ben and Ruben, for the timeliest of interventions, and to
Mum and Dad for their tireless support and refusal to discourage
their children (even though it has been said that I have been
a nightmare of a child).

This edition first published in Canada in 2004 by Whitecap Books, 351 Lynn Ave.,
North Vancouver, British Columbia, Canada, V7J 2C4.

www.whitecap.ca

First published in 2004 by Murdoch Books®, a division of Murdoch Magazines Pty Ltd.

Design Concept: Marylouise Brammer
Designer: Vivien Valk
Photographer: Alan Benson
Stylist: Sarah de Nardi
Editorial Director: Diana Hill
Editors: Sarah Baker and Diana Hill
Production: Megan Alsop

Printed by Midas Printing (Asia) Ltd. PRINTED IN CHINA.

ISBN 1-55285-628-3

First printed 2004. Text, photography and design © Murdoch Books 2004.

flowers
at home

mariella ienna

whitecap

contents

floral anarchy

My great love is for foliage rather than flowers. I often spend the first hour or so on buying days at the markets looking at leaves and other interesting green forms. I read somewhere that 'verdant is the interface between us and nature', and this quote really appeals to me as it is the overriding philosphy for what I do. For me, designing and composing arrangements has been an outlet for filtering and putting together natural forms without those forms being too contrived — or necessarily 'floral' for that matter.

Some people complain that flowers die too quickly, but there is beauty in natural transience. Appreciate things for what they are, not what they should be. If you have an eye for forms, textures, colours and shapes, then you can put together objects of beauty. Treat foliage as an integral part of each arrangement, not as a 'filler'. Trust your instincts about what your own environment requires — after all, you are the one who will be living with those branches, leaves and flowers for a day or a week.

When arranging flowers and foliage, use one or two colours only: use a single stem, leaf or branch as selectively as you would a fashion accessory. Indeed, if you have a keen fashion eye, think of coordinating flowers as you would your wardrobe.

I have found that there are laws of nature that affect how well arrangements come together. Let me use the fashion analogy. Mere mortals wouldn't get away with wearing a beautifully cut tweed suit with an Hawaiian shirt; in the same way, a ginger flower does not go well with, say, a gardenia. One is tropical in style and the other is classical.

So look at the textures of flowers and foliage as well as the style that they represent — whether tropical, cottagey, native, classical or fragrant. Treat them as if they were the fabric, cut and style of a piece of clothing, capable of creating a distinctive look and sense of occasion. This is how I begin to assess how flowers and foliage might harmoniously mingle, and it is the only analogy that helps me to bring some logic to the process. As with all aesthetic enterprises, it is mainly an instinctive one.

And, finally, here are some practical tips to bear in mind. Do keep an eye out for beautiful and diverse vases and objects to hold flowers and foliage: an intrinsic part of an arrangement is the vessel that contains it and the relationship between all of the elements in your composition. And make sure that your vessels are always clean; a dirty vase is one of the few grim things in the beautiful world of flowers.

Avoid senseless use of floral foam and wires. Work with the natural flow and posture of your materials.

Give your flowers and foliage fresh drinks of water as often as possible, and trim their stems to help them drink and live with you for as long as they can. Never let the water in the vase become dirty.

Oh...and less is always more. But by the same token, do mix styles; be adventurous. You can always pull it all apart and start again — such fun — if it doesn't work the first time. Create and destroy! I suppose I sound like a floral anarchist. There could be something in that.

vanity fair

feminine, sexy and chic —
modern and sharp

elements

Simply, camellias. At the end of winter, camellia trees come to life, their delicate and feminine blooms giving a stunning display of colours and petal formations, which are highlighted in this arrangement. Mixed open peony roses, or open ranunculus, would also look great in this style.

vase type

To contrast with and emphasize the feminine voluptuousness of the open camellias and their glossy green foliage, choose simple, clear glass forms. For the arrangement shown here, choose bud vases of varying sizes. Square, elongated and squat forms work best. Round glass forms are less effective, as they are too similar in shape to the camellia flower and provide less of a contrast in shape and form.

method

The focus in this arrangement is on collecting an array of colours and petal varieties. Camellia colours range from white and pale pink, through mottled patterned hot pinks and whites, to dark pinky reds, so if a variety of camellias is available to you, select one or two blooms from each tree.

Trim the stems — a clean, sharp cut with secateurs is the best method — and immediately place them in water (if only in a jug or small bucket prior to arranging). Fill the vases with water and arrange the flowers randomly.

The eye should also be drawn to the beautiful woodiness of the camellia stem, which is in rustic contrast to the obvious prettiness of the blooms. If you criss-cross the stems (especially when using elongated vases), the arrangement assumes the appearance of a suspended dancer, pirouetting. If you want the arrangement to last longer than a day or two, select camellia buds and partly opened camellias as opposed to fully open ones, which will drop within a day or two of opening. You will find that nearly open flowers will take a day to unfurl. Tight buds, on the other hand, may take a week to open.

It may be worth washing the woody stems before arranging them in the glass vases, as they can often shed small barky bits that float in the water, spoiling the effect.

'miss havisham'

quirky tea party with an edge; high artifice — flowers like exquisitely dressed coquettes

elements Light-coloured camellias. Choose white or pale pink blooms that are quite thick-petalled (double-petalled preferably), as the petals must withstand a coating of floral paint, sprayed from a can. You can purchase these sprays from florist supply shops as well as art suppliers. Peony roses or very open David Austin roses would also look fantastic in this style.

vase type Beautiful, intricate and decorative. Try to avoid really pink and over-the-top feminine vases, which are rather clichéd and shabby chic. Instead, look for less obvious quirks in your vessel, such as gold or pearlescent shimmers, odd handles and feet or embossed and high-relief details.

method Floral spray is a special form of spray paint suitable for using on flowers. Many of the colours are gaudy and inappropriate; however, there are some fabulous effects to be obtained by using floral paint subtly. Try 'gold shimmer' or 'shimmer pearly dew', both of which provide, of course, a shimmer effect.

Spray the flowers outdoors and away from other objects. Hold each flower by the stem at arm's length and spray lightly. Commence with very light applications of paint and build up with more applications of spray, if required. When spraying, aim for a light dusting, rather than a solid coating of colour.

Arrange the flowers as for 'vanity fair', page 16.

Spray paint the flowers on the day that you are using them. This arrangement will not look its best after a day or two: it is more suited to a one-off use for a party or other special occasion.

It is quite nice to leave brown woody bits on the stems, such as those on these silver leaves. Such small features can add interest, especially when they are magnified under the water line. Make sure that they don't muddy the water, however: rinse them thoroughly and rub them to remove any flaky bits. Dirty stems not only look unattractive, they will also accelerate the deterioration of the water as well as the flowers and foliage.

With its copious display of petals and downy leaves, this arrangement
is soft and feminine. Position the leaves so that they spill over the
rim of the vase and soften it.

vanille

sublimely pastelly, silvery, velvety

elements   Peonies and senecio. When buying peonies, or any flowers that
commence as tight buds, you can be pleasantly surprised by a
chance purchase of blooms that hide a second petal colour at
their inner core. This arrangement is very simple in order to
enhance the two-toned nature of the peony petals. Silver foliage
(such as that of the senecio shown here) accompanies pastel
colours especially well, and the silver leaves in this
arrangement have a gorgeous downy, tactile appeal.

vase type   A tall, elegant, clear glass vase suits the composition best, as
the stems of the peonies also form part of the composition. This
shape seems to look particularly good with arrangements that are
top-heavy. You could also use a very simple, tall cylindrical
vase. Coloured glass would detract from the subtlety of the pink,
cream and silver colours of the flowers and foliage.

method   Fill the vase with enough water to capture both the peony stems
and the shorter stems of the silver foliage. Strip the peony
stems of all foliage, except for the smaller leaves around the
buds themselves. It is important to the composition that there
not be too much of a mixture of silver and green foliage. The
colours are so subtle in this arrangement that too much green
foliage will detract from the pink, cream and silver.

Position the bunches of peonies together, vertically across the
vase, in one group. If you like, some of the peonies can be
higher than the others. The stems should all be positioned in the
same direction too. Then add the silver foliage, below the
peonies and filling the remaining space at the base of the vase.

winsome

the humble perfection of real roses and berries in sepia-washed tones

elements Roses and berries. 'Julia's Rose', an old-style garden rose, has a tea-stained colour with a surprising warm golden centre and pronounced golden stamens. All David Austin roses have old-world allure, most with perfume. Growers cut them so that the smaller ancillary buds are left intact (as if picked from the garden). They open beautifully.

Try to avoid those rose buds that come in monotonous generic clusters, with sad little heads that have no hope of maturing and opening, inevitably drooping after a day or two — robbed of their true potential by mass production. Ask the growers at markets how they grow their roses and educate yourself about the different varieties. It opens up a world of new choices and in my view, vase longevity.

Roses look beautiful with berries. These cute snowberries (*Symphoricarpus* species) are available at the end of summer, but any berries (even edible berries such as mulberries, raspberries, strawberries) would be appealing. Incorporate the berry foliage into the design too.

Berries can last for weeks in a vase as they slowly dehydrate (looking quite good dried), but their leaves always let them down by starting to go brown and/or dry up within days. So save yourself the trouble and strip them all off. Also, watch out for fruit flies, which can rapidly spoil the arrangement. And extend the life of your roses by changing the water daily and recutting the stems in the process.

vase type   A small low bowl in earthenware or glazed pottery will add to
             the charm of this arrangement. The surface of this gorgeous
             little pottery bowl has the most delicate textural imprint of
             lace. The design of the vessel can add to the mood created by
             the flowers with all their intricate details. Even a quirky
             little tarnished silver teapot would look great filled with
             'Julia's Rose', as would a two-handled sugar bowl in a soft
             glaze. Avoid vessels with too many flowery prints (such as those
             pictured with the 'miss havisham' design, page 20, where the pink
             of the flowers is strong enough to carry a highly patterned
             vessel): this will detract from the subtle colours of the roses
             and berries.

method   Fill the vase with water and strip the rose stems of any leaves
             that would be submerged. Don't strip the thorns off with rose
             strippers or the like: this is very harsh and seems to damage
             the stems in the process, so that they become prematurely icky
             and slimy after a day or so in the water. Recut the stems of the
             roses vertically and place them in water immediately. You might
             have to cut them quite short so that they balance properly in a
             low, squat open bowl. Arrange the roses so that they spill over
             the side of the bowl, in an uneven fashion, but make sure that
             the stems stay in water. It can be a little tricky with this
             style of container. Don't arrange the roses too evenly; in fact,
             if you like, arrange the bulk of the roses on one side of the
             vase and the berries on the other side.

             Strip the berries, removing most of the leaves. Arrange the
             berries on top of the roses, or off to one side. To secure the
             arrangement, use the weight of the berry stems to help anchor the
             roses in place, particularly if you use a low, squat vase.
             Otherwise they might fall out, due to the heaviness of the rose
             flower and lack of support afforded by the vase shape.

madam butterfly

an extravagance of petals, a bravura performance

elements   Masses of white peonies, basically. Buy peonies as tight buds. Even if they are very small, these buds usually grow for one to two days after they have been cut. Feminine and pure, white peonies sometimes secrete hot pink-tipped petals at their inner core. And peonies have lovely green foliage too, so use them to full effect in your arrangements.

vase type   A mass of white blooms looks good in any style of vase. This one in clear glass is a modern take on the stem vase, but with more angular, elongated shapes. This balances the roundness of the peonies and their unfurling petals. Use any vase that is not round like a fishbowl, otherwise the arrangement could look altogether too spherical. An oriental-style tall vase would also look lovely, and would play up the significance of the peony as the national flower of China. Avoid vases with very small openings, as they will not accommodate lots of peony stems.

method   Cut the stems vertically and strip the peony stems of leaves that would be submerged once in the vase. Fill the vase with water, and arrange the peonies in the vessel. If the peonies are still at the tight bud stage, try not to overlap them too much as they will need a fair amount of room in which to open. Because the arrangement is so simple, consider the significance of the green foliage at the opening of the vase. The leaves can be used to cascade over the rim and soften any harsh lines. The dark green then becomes an important addition to the composition. It's as if the flowers are wearing a green shawl.

If any peony flowers snap off, or need further support once opened (due to the heaviness of their petals), strip their stems and use the blooms in a float bowl for a special table arrangement. They will last a day or two.

The fine foliage on the woody rubia stems will spoil the water very quickly, so strip off as much as you can.

A warning: don't be tempted to eat the seeds that are still on the sunflower head, as they must be dried properly first.

orb

circles within circles within...

elements

Rubia pods, sunflower seed heads (*Helianthus* species) and fatsia leaves (*Fatsia japonica*). The rubia shrub blooms throughout summer with pods that are usually green, but there is also a less common variety that has a very large head and grey/white pods, with luminous deep red stems. Once cut, the pods are long lasting and dry very well, although their vibrant green and red colours fade. When the sunflower begins to drop its petals, the green fringing around the massive seed head maintains its limey green, a perfect frame for a big orb bulging with black sunflower seeds. When incorporated into arrangements, this orb, without petals, holds more interest than the yellow-petalled flower. Finally, the large fan-shaped fatsia leaves are always a good finishing touch to any arrangement because of their colour, lustre, shape and durability.

vase type

A rustic grey stone garden urn with a stem base is a strong, understated vessel, whose classical curves draw out the repetitive round shapes of the rubia pods and sunflower orbs. Grey vessels seem to complement vivid green colours very well. Again, depending on the mood that you wish to create and the nature of your interior, don't be afraid to mix apparently unlikely combinations of flowers and vessels. It is important to recognize the scale and impact of your materials; this arrangement would look out of place — and out of proportion — in a small vase.

method

If you are using a stone or cement urn, place a plastic container filled with water inside as it will probably not be watertight. Position the fatsia leaves at the back of the arrangement first, using the rim of the urn to support the leaves. Strip the sunflower stems of any foliage and then add the sunflower heads to the foreground, but off to one side in a cluster. Keep the rubia stems long and add them to the urn in clusters, positioning them so that they spill over the urn rim.

russet

warm tones of earth and autumn,
        textures of bark, berries and leaves

elements   Eucalyptus bark, rosehips, *Pittosporum rhombifolium* (rumbo) berries,
            echinacea, dwarf sacred bamboo leaves (*Nandina domestica*) and
            assorted autumn foliage. Thick shards of eucalyptus bark, which you
            can easily collect from the base of large trees, form the base of
            this table-setting design.

vase type   Organic dried materials such as bark, palm husks (see the
            'succulence' design, page 154) and driftwood (see the 'driftwood'
            design, page 110), are readily available as natural vessels, and
            may be even more appropriate than a conventional glass vase,
            depending upon the elements and mood and feel of the overall
            design. In this arrangement, the woody base of the bark
            accentuates the warm, inviting and predominantly autumnal feel of
            rosehips, orange rumbo berries, orange echinacea and a variety of
            loose deciduous foliage.

method   Lay the shards of bark down the centre of your dinner table, or
            in a low mound if your table is circular (but it shouldn't be so
            high that it begins to resemble a campfire). Brush any grit from
            the bark before you lay the table, particularly if you are using
            a tablecloth; dirt and grit do not complement an otherwise
            immaculate white tablecloth. Lay the leaves among the bark,
            ensuring that the stems are facing down towards the table, with
            the foliage emerging above the bark. Finish the arrangement by
            placing clusters of berries and rosehips among the leaves.

            If you have some rosehips left over, place them on dinner plates
            or tie them around table napkins as a complementary gesture. For a
            place card, tie a small tag to a cluster of rosehips.

No water is required for this arrangement, as it is designed to be used for a one-off occasion such as a dinner or lunch. The foliage and berries should last for some days out of water and maintain their colours, before beginning to dry and fade.

After the dinner party, rearrange clusters of bark, leaves and berries in a low bowl. If you are able to recut the stems of the leaves and place them in water at this stage, you will prolong their drying and fading process.

stix

exaggeratedly, starkly organic;
sculptural in its simplicity

elements

Ginger stems and immature palm seed pods. Many tropical flowering ginger varieties have beautiful patterned stems. When cut, these are known in floristry as ginger sticks. The brown and green striped patterns on the sticks seem to have been painted on; if you look closely, the colour can appear to have been applied with an airbrush. You can also find strange variations, such as kneebone-shaped sticks with dark and light green mottled patterns. Palm trees are another source of material. Young palm seed pods that have not yet cracked open have a gorgeous browny ochre colour and a sharp, spear-like appearance. For a tribal yet modern and quirky look, bring subtle-coloured and patterned sticks such as these together.

Use a tall, clear glass vase for this arrangement if you want a modern effect with a quirky edge.

The ginger sticks are likely to last two or three months out of water before their stems begin to deteriorate. Palm seed pods, on the other hand, will dry and retain their shape permanently.

vase type   You can go two ways with this arrangement — either the more conventional rustic vessel, such as a rough, unglazed pottery vase (which will give the arrangement more of a tribal feel), or a tall, clear glass vase as shown on page 39.

method   Simply mix up the patterned sticks and arrange them in the vessel as you see fit. The sticks will be shown to even better effect if you use a clear glass vessel, placed in a light-filled position.

If you have some shorter sticks, bundle them together with strips made from palm fronds, and use them to decorate a doorstep or table.

pod

textures and patterns created by the nurturing of new life

elements

Poinsettia pods (*Euphorbia pulcherrima*) and ice-cream beans (*Inga edulis*). In warm climates, many tropical trees drop seed pods that come in a multitude of interesting shapes and sizes, and that also dry well. For this arrangement, gather spectacularly long poinsettia pods, which resemble polished wood, and green pods, commonly known as ice-cream beans. (Apparently, the contents of the fresh seeds contained within the pod taste like ice-cream, although we do not recommend that you test this theory.)

vase type

Use a low, round or elongated vessel, in ceramic or wire, like the basket in this arrangement. A dark vessel (black or charcoal or dark olive green) will emphasize the predominantly dark brown and green colours of the seed pods. Or, for an interesting twist, display them vertically in a very simple, tall, clear glass vase.

method

Arrange the seed pods, vertically or horizontally, to suit your vessel. Distinguish the fresher seeds from the dried ones, and selectively disperse open seeds with patterns and textures as if they were highlights of the collection.

This arrangement will last forever and should evolve as a collection in progress. To refresh it, switch vessels (from the horizontal arrangement in a low bowl to a vertical arrangement in a tall glass vase) and enjoy the seeds anew from different angles. As you find them, add fresh seeds to your sculptural collection.

Crack the seed pods open to expose interiors textured and patterned by the process of nurturing seeds.

grasslands

the strong verticality of fresh
        green stalks transforms into the
arching elegance of dried foliage

elements   Mondo grass (*Ophiopogon* species), sedge (*Carex* 'Frosted Curls'),
saviour grass (*Dasypogon bromeliifolius*) and zebra grass
(*Miscanthus sinensis* 'Zebrinus'). Amazingly versatile, grasses have
a simple and undeniable sculptural appeal. Here are two grass
arrangements, one dried and one fresh, which demonstrate how you
can literally throw together vertical strands of green and brown to
create simple yet striking beauty in your home. For the fresh
arrangement (opposite), use a variety of tall, green ornamental
mondo grass. This is quite a vivid, minimal and fresh look. For
the dried arrangement (see page 46), aim for a more sophisticated
and elegant feel by playing on muted colour and dried textures. In
this arrangement, tall and sinuous zebra grass is combined with a
brown straw-like sorghum grass.

The simpler the arrangement, the more the vessel becomes the focus.
The austerity of these fresh grasses makes your choice of vase a
critical element in the mood you create.

There is a huge variety of grasses, and in most cases, you can enjoy them fresh as well as in their various phases of drying. For instance, the tall mondo grass used in the fresh arrangement on page 45 looks increasingly spectacular as it begins to dry into muted green curls. These can even be used in *très élégant* wedding bouquets!

vase type   When using fresh grasses, select very simple, clear glass vases.
Vases with a pattern, such as the ribbed vase shown on page 45,
work well: a play on the vertical and horizontal lines provides
further interest. You can also repeat this very simple effect by
using several vases.

For the dried arrangement, a vessel in a muted, natural hue will
complement the faded tones of the grasses. You could also be
adventurous with the vessel shape, as the dried grasses have
twists, curves, curls and textures that invite a more
sophisticated approach to the composition. Do avoid patterns and
bright colours that will distract the eye from the subtleties of
the dried grasses.

method   You can prolong the greenness of the fresh grasses by adding
water to the vase before you arrange the material. Alternatively,
simply let the grass 'morph' into its dried state.

For the dried arrangement, arrange each type of dried grass in
clusters in the vase. As simple as that.

Plastic vials can be
used in a sneaky way:
they allow you to place
flowers or leaves
virtually anywhere in
your home (see page 72).
The same thing could be
done with an ornate
mirror, lamp base
or bedhead.

luxe

decadent and luxurious flowers;
opulence in looks and in fragrance

elements
: *Magnolia grandiflora* 'Little Gem', *Cattleya* orchids and stephanotis. The basis of this arrangement is the foliage and buds of the magnolia 'Little Gem'. If you can't get this magnolia, try *Michelia yunnanensis*. Buy tight buds, and handle them with care: the buds bruise very easily. Once open, the flower has a beautiful citrus fragrance. The foliage of this variety of magnolia is as beautiful as the flower — rich, dark green and glossy, with an underside of luscious downy velvet. The flowers of the *Cattleya* orchid range from small to very large cabbagey blooms. When especially large (as in plate size), they become a little tricky to handle, as they are quite floppy. This orchid has an unexpected fragrance, which is quite subtle and delicate. Trailing stephanotis vine, with its thick, sturdy stem and clusters of fragrant flowers, adds to the lushness of this composition. If you cannot obtain it, use another creeping vine with flowers that are a little out of the ordinary. Don't use ivy or jasmine: they don't suit the precious tone set by the other flowers.

vase type
: All the flowers used in this arrangement have a decadent and luxurious quality. The vase too should accentuate the mood set by the flowers and foliage. A clear glass stem vase is ideal. Stem vases in general make any arrangement look good, but they particularly suit a trailing composition (and here the stephanotis vine can be used to its full cascading effect). Alternatively, a tall, clear glass vase will work just as well.

The magnolia leaves will outlive all the other
elements in this arrangement, so retain them after
the flowers are gone and enjoy them a little longer
in a bowl or another type of short vase.

method

Remove all the magnolia leaves at the base of the stem that will
be submerged or they will quickly muddy the water. Arrange 1-3
magnolia bunches to cover the opening of the vase. If you are
fortunate enough to have found *Cattleya* orchids with long stems,
place them in clusters off to one side of the arrangement,
depending on whether it is to be viewed from one side only.
Otherwise disperse them, preferably in clusters throughout.

The orchids are more likely to have short stems which cannot
reach the water, given the extent of the foliage in the
arrangement. Either make room at the mouth of the vessel by
parting the magnolia stems, or use plastic vials of water (see
page 72). Place the vials containing the orchids in the magnolia
foliage. In this way, short-stemmed orchids can sit quite high in
the arrangement, above the water line. Make sure you top up the
water regularly.

Have some fun with the stephanotis trails by wrapping them around
the vase; the stem of the vase will hold these particularly well.
You can even soften the line of the vase by covering the entire
composition with foliage. Or twine stephanotis around surrounding
ornamentation or architectural elements once the vase is *in situ*.

This arrangement should last at least a week, the combined
perfume of all its elements overpowering you. You can prolong it
by cutting out magnolia buds that have opened to a flower and
begun to decay.

ruby

rouge et noir; darkly mysterious and elegant

elements
Hippeastrums, red umbrella top spikes (*Schefflera actinophylla*) and black philodendron leaves. Look for full, bursting hippeastrum buds on tall, thick, strong and undamaged stems. Buy ruby red umbrella top flower spikes. Handle these spikes with care, as the flower nodules are easily damaged and can fall off. Dramatic black philodendron leaves last for weeks in a vase.

vase type
Two complementary vessels work well with a split composition. Choose two vases — one tall and one squat. One can be more ornate and the other simpler if you like; combining clear and coloured (red) glass will also add interest. Choose glass vessels with some old-world charm and sophistication to them.

method
Fill the vessels with water, and separate taller umbrella top spikes from the shorter ones. To shorten the spikes, measure the stem length against the appropriate tall or short vessel. Remove flower nodules from the stem that will be submerged. Then cut the stem down vertically to a shorter length. Arrange the taller spikes off to one side (grouped together) in the taller vase, then do the same with the shorter spikes in the squat vase.

Separate the opening or open hippeastrum buds from those that are still closed. Arrange the buds in the shorter vase, and the open flowers in the taller vase, cutting the stems vertically to the right length. The flowers should sit roughly a quarter of their total length above the lip of the vase, given that they are quite trumpet-like when they open, but they can be a little taller if you like. Look at the relationship between the hippeastrums and the spikes, and cut the flowers down (or up) accordingly. Also, arrange the hippeastrums in the composition so that they sit facing in the opposite direction to the spikes. Finish the vases by placing the philodendron leaves above the lip of the vases, in a fan-like manner.

About five days after cutting, the umbrella top spikes will fade to a burgundy brown, and they will dry quite well. But once they have dried, they can be a little messy if you knock them. Place the spikes in a vase (without water) to aid the drying process and position them out of harm's way (or else have a vacuum cleaner handy).

55

purple haze

glamorous formality on a lavish scale

elements

Celosia, smoke bush foliage (*Cotinus coggygria*), dyed black pheasant feathers and carnations (*Dianthus* species). Celosia has a flower head comprised of curling, velvety florets. It is a luscious flower that is unrivalled in its tactile appeal. Celosia comes in a rainbow of colours, and has attractive, tender green foliage. Look for sturdy stems and big flower heads, and avoid limp dehydrated leaves that are already on their way out. Purple smoke bush leaves seem to naturally complement celosia.

The double-petalled varieties of carnation are quite gorgeous: a number of bunches together of the same colour can easily be mistaken for peonies. They last more than two weeks in a vase.

vase type

The size of the arrangement and the dark colours used require a tall, dark vase, preferably in a dark-coloured glass. Alternatively, a tall, black metal urn with handles or an oriental-shaped glazed vase, again in a dark colour, would be suitable.

method

Fill the vase with water and place it *in situ* if the vase is especially large. Strip the smoke bush of foliage and any flower heads at the base of the stem that will be submerged, and cut the stems vertically prior to positioning them in two groups on either side of the vase. Then, place the celosia, stripped of all leaves, with stems cut vertically, in the centre of the vase, framed by the smoke bush foliage. Add the carnations, making use of their long, thin, tall stems to insert them in between the celosia and one cluster of the smoke bush foliage. The carnations should sit above the celosia as a distinctive feature. Finally, position the feathers. Place the vase near a natural light source so that the dark glass is illuminated.

The foliage of the celosia flower does tend to die off quickly and make an arrangement look shabby (even though the flower head can look great for two weeks), so strip off the leaves and mix the flower heads with other foliage.

Keep the feathers in the
vase and change the
foliage that you add to
the arrangement. Avoid
wetting the feathers as
they can lose their
shape or, worse, look
like they've been permed.

plume

soft and light and tickly;
wonderfully whimsical

elements Any kind of fluffy, bushy, plumy foliage and feathers of a similar texture. The foliage shouldn't be so dense that it overwhelms the lightness of the feathers. I've used a taller, upright variety of asparagus fern (*Protasparagus* species). Drying, curly grasses also work well (see 'grasslands', page 44).

Try to collect wonderful feathers as you find them — either in nature or from costume stores and specialist feather sellers. Natural-toned feathers work best with foliage because the subtle hues, shapes and textures of both elements emulate one another. Stripy or patterned natural-coloured feathers would also look fantastic. The arrangement is powerful in its restraint; you should avoid brightly coloured feathers that would make it all look a bit vaudevillian.

vase type Given the simplicity of the arrangement, a strong yet quirky vessel really enhances the overall composition. A large, tall vessel with words or images, such as the one pictured, or one with a pattern, such as black and white stripes, would also look amazing. If you find an interesting-shaped vessel that is neutral in tone, this will also work; again, avoid bright colours.

method Fill the vase with enough water to cover the stems of the foliage. Avoid wetting the feathers in any way. Don't spread the feathers and foliage out too much, rather arrange them in clumps. Because the feathers are likely to be curved at their tip, arrange them so that they arch towards you from the vase.

gilt

ethereal waxen flowers
amid a filigree of
lacey, gilded branches

elements
Gilded magnolia branches and *Phalaenopsis* orchids. You can purchase magnolia branches that are bare, in leaf with fluffy buds or flowering at the flower markets from time to time, especially at the end of winter when many varieties of the magnolia tree flower. In early spring look for pruned cuttings, which gardeners often leave out for green waste collection. The branches can seem amazingly deformed, especially if they have grown in the shade.

Phalaenopsis orchids are sublime creatures, with patterned throats and odd little beards. Commonly known as moth orchids, they seem to hover above stems and roots. Frequently appearing in interior design magazines, the cut flowers are also very popular in wedding arrangements because they are simply elegance on a stem. And that is why you should not add too much to the *Phalaenopsis* orchid. Clean white orchids and gilded bare branches are the perfect foil for each other.

vase type
Select a clear and elegant vase with some decorative elements, such as the blown glass with gold glitter flecks pictured. Otherwise modern, clean shapes would work well. Clear glass is best for showing off the detail of the branches and the curve of the orchid stems. Choose the glassware according to the height and formation of the magnolia branches.

Magnolia branches dry perfectly and are really quite versatile in the effects that they can evoke — for example, you can achieve quite a romantic look by coupling sparse branches with pretty petalled flowers and foliage. Try roses and camellia leaves.

Using your finger, apply a fine film of gilding wax paste to select branches and even orchid stems.

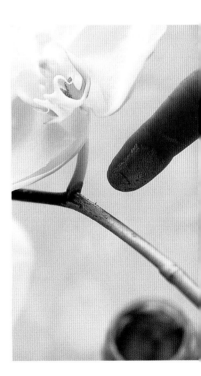

When arranging, be careful not to let the branches slice through the very delicate petals of the orchid. The branches can be sharp enough to cut the petals, a tragedy when it occurs.

method   Fill the vase with enough water to capture the orchid stems. Ideally, the branches should not be submerged, so if you can, position these well above the water line. However, if the branches have some greenery on them, such as the young leaves shown in this arrangement, then they should be partly submerged to keep the foliage fresh. When positioning the branches, take into consideration the shape and proportions of the vase and the number of stems of orchids. One significant magnolia branch may be enough, or a number of smaller branches may be more appropriate. The branches should complement, not overwhelm, the orchids. Place the orchid stems between the branches towards the front of the arrangement (if there is a front), or at key focal points.

To gild the magnolia branches, use a small pot of gilding wax paste, which you can purchase from art suppliers. Dip your finger in the paste and apply a fine film of gold to some of the magnolia branches and orchid stems. Use it sparingly. There is no point in buying gold leaf to do the gilding, as this is expensive; gilding wax paste is cheap and produces the same bright gold effect. This arrangement would look great in an interior where there is an element of gilt furniture, such as a hall table with a gilt mirror. Or it could be used as a contrasting feature in a modern, sparse, white interior, or as a formal and special occasion arrangement, such as table settings for a wedding.

edgy

cinderella

an adult fairytale; sugary pink
meets shadowy shades

elements *Dendrobium* and *Cattleya* orchids, belladonna lilies (*Amaryllis belladonna*) and alocasia leaves. A single orchid combined with a beautiful leaf, or even a feather, can seem like the trimming on an amazing hat. Mix darker shades of orchid stems with deep velvet green, variegated alocasia leaves. And you may wish to give an arrangement of short-stemmed clusters of orchids some height by adding sculptural flower buds. Choose the colours of the buds to tone with the colours of the orchids. The pinky brown orchids in this arrangement complement the milk chocolate stems of the belladonna lilies and the creamy membrane that contains the pale pink, fragrant petals.

vase type Use two vases for these flowers. Choose coloured translucent glass in pinks, browns or dark greens to tone in with the colours of the orchid blooms and leaves. At the very least one should be tall and one low, to suit the varying sizes of the orchid, bud and leaf stems.

method Fill the tall vase with water and cut the stems of the belladonna buds, then arrange them in a cluster off to one side. Add taller and larger alocasia leaves, perhaps only two or three, to the base of this vase. As you arrange the leaves and the belladonna buds, be conscious of the pointy tips of these leaves in relation to the tips of the buds. Depending on how many orchid stems you have, fill one or two low vases with water. Arrange the orchid stems first, cutting each one before placing it in water. If you can, spill the orchids over the side of the low vase. Place the low vase *in situ* with the tall vase, and finish the low vase with its share of alocasia leaves.

Sets or clusters of vases in a similar style are useful design tools: they can heighten the interest in your arrangements, and as the blooms change, you can move individual vases to other locations.

The beauty of this arrangement is that you can keep the dried components in place and change the fresh elements each week (similar to the 'lichen' design, page 122.)

chiaroscuro

creating drama with the interplay
of light and shade

elements Yucca flower spikes, lotus leaves (*Nelumbo* species), Moreton Bay fig aerial roots (*Ficus macrophylla*) and any kind of dramatically shaped dried sticks. This arrangement is quite a *tour de force* of dramatic composition, evoking *film noir* images. Chiaroscuro is a term used in the context of fine art or cinematography to describe images that capture light and dark extremes of form and colour. For the 'light' colour and 'soft' texture components of this design, use creamy lime flower spikes cut from the yucca plant and the bizarre shapes of faded green, partially dried lotus leaves. If you are unable to get the creamy yucca flowers, use buds of white Asiatic hybrid liliums, which will look just as good once they are open. Cream or green gladioli spikes might work too. For the 'dark' colour and 'hard' textural components, use dried sticks (the ones pictured have been dyed black) and a creepy Moreton Bay fig aerial root, with weepy tendrils. A fantastic alternative to dyed sticks are the black claw-like flowers of *Phormium* 'Sea Jade', a New Zealand flax.

vase type   Again, a cluster of similar vases is used in quite an overt manner
in this design; this device isolates the mix of dried and fresh
organic components. Find a set of at least four vases, in charcoal
or black, and in varying sizes and heights. Because the design of
this arrangement is intricate and dramatic, stick to dark vessels
without a pattern, such as ceramics with textures. The amazing
black rubber vessels pictured are made out of recycled car tyres.

method   Arrange each of the light and dark components in each vase. The
only vase requiring water is the one containing the creamy lime
yucca spikes (if you purchase these when they are in bud, the
buds will open into flowers and last over a week). Arrange the
vases and chiaroscuro components as you please; however, you may
wish to add the Moreton Bay fig root last, as it is likely to be
the most dramatic element in the arrangement. The curve of its
tendrils should form an eerie arc over the other elements. Do
resist the urge to always position the fresh 'pretty' flowers so
that they are the focus of the arrangement. Indeed, place that
vase in the background, or off to the side, and see how the
light colours illuminate the darker elements in the foreground,
as if they were backlit.

Be aware of another effect of this sculptural arrangement
— the dramatic shadows it casts on the surrounding walls.

Cut orchids should be sold in plastic
vials, so you may already have some of
these. If not, buy some from a floral
supply store.

rooted

look for beauty beyond the obvious,
waiting for you below the surface

elements   Crucifix orchids (*Epidendrum* species) and their roots. Crucifix
orchids really have it all — a long, elegant stem with thick,
lustrous green leaves at its base, and at its head, a cluster of
individual two-tone orchids in a crucifix shape. The older stems
sprout new stems and roots. Keep these orchid roots intact and
make them part of the arrangement, emphasizing them by using
additional orchid roots (see the 'spike' design, page 162). Or
try light and ethereal 'old man's beard' or Spanish moss foliage
(*Tillandsia usneoides*), a miraculous hanging epiphytic foliage
that survives on air and water misting alone.

vase type   With the focus of this arrangement on roots and root shapes,
a tall, clear glass vase is the best choice. It will support the
tall stems of the orchids as well as showcase the composition
below the vase neck.

method   Arrange the dry orchid roots or old man's beard inside the vase.
Fill a quarter to a half of the vase with this nesty effect. If
the orchid stems are short, don't go overboard with the height and
density of the root effect, or the roots will overwhelm the
lightness of the orchid stems. Finally, insert the stems of the
crucifix orchids into plastic vials, as shown above, and position
the stems in the vase, hiding the vials in the orchid roots.

Crucifix orchids are
epiphytic — that is, they
grow on other plants
without being parasitic.

73

gnarled

nature twisted, contorted, warped,
woven and plaited into imperfect elegance

elements Rather than restrict wreaths to Christmas time, why not regard them as yet another structure upon which to display flowers and foliage? Wreaths make a wonderful welcome gesture on the front door and gate of your home. You can buy gnarled vine, tamed and twisted into round shapes, at the flower markets and from craft shops, or you could prune thick pieces of dried palm frond, wisteria or bougainvillea from your own garden.

method While they are still green, freshly cut wisteria and bougainvillea vines should be easy enough to shape. If they prove resistant, soak the pieces in water overnight to make them malleable and flexible. Start your basic wreath structure by tying two or three large pieces of the vine together with fine wire, then add other finer pieces of vine, also securing them with wire. Then gradually weave them through the attached vine so that they are self-supporting and stay in place as the wreath begins to thicken and take shape.

Alternatively, twist dried palm fronds into a round shape. First, snap the thick spine that runs down the centre of each leaf in three or four places. Do not snap the frond into separate pieces.

A pretty wreath made with
Plectranthus oertendahlii and leaves of
Fijian fire bush (*Acalypha* species).

Place candles in low glass containers
and encircle them with wreaths.

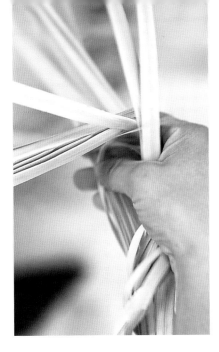

Make a wreath by weaving dried
palm fronds together.

Opposite, clockwise from top
left, wreaths made from:
ornamental ginger, guava
(*Psidium* species) and gold-back
fern (*Pentagramma* species);
orchids, buttonhole hosta
leaves and feathers; rosehips
and autumn leaves; silver
acacia and tetra nuts
(*Eucalyptus tetrodonta*).

Rather, bend the spine in those positions so that the fibres are
stretched, allowing the frond to be twisted. Twist the length
into a circle and secure it with fine wire. Bulk up the palm
circle into a plump wreath by weaving loose pieces of dried palm
leaf through the wreath.

Combine flowers, foliage, fruits, feathers and nuts into wreaths.
Some ideas are shown opposite.

In all but one of the wreaths, you should be able to weave the
elements through the structure without using any wire or tape.
Use the loose woven gaps in the wreath structure to contain and
secure your flowers and foliage. It is as simple as that. In the
orchid, hosta leaf and feather wreath (pictured opposite, top
right), you will need a little bit of wire to keep the
individual short-stemmed orchids in place. Bear in mind that
fresh wreaths made from wisteria or bougainvillea will shrink as
they dehydrate. Secure your flowers and foliage with wire or
twine if necessary.

The rosy little fruits of the crab apple.

florid

voluptuous, indulgent, but all class — abandon moderation

elements
Pink flowers, crab apple branches (*Malus* species), *Tradescantia pallida* 'Purple Heart' and large tropical leaves. Choose lots of blooms in diverse yet classical shapes — open David Austin roses, Parrot tulips, tiger lilies, hydrangeas. The one anchor is colour. To give this arrangement of pink flowers a mixture of interesting shapes and textures, use crab apple branches (with little fruits) for height, the fleshy purple foliage of tradescantia to nestle among the petalled flowers, and large, vivid green, pointed leaves that will lend a cascading effect. The foliage will break up the 'prettiness' of the petals.

vase type
A large, black metal, stemmed urn will also redeem the profusion of petals, and emphasize the shapes of the trailing purple tradescantia in particular, visually slicing through them.

method
Most metal urns do not hold water, so insert a plastic container filled with water. Arrange the tall crab apple branches at the back of the arrangement first; let their height mirror the height of the stem of the urn. Then add the large tropical leaves to the front and sides of the arrangement, letting some hang down over the front to soften the line of the stem. Add clusters of your chosen blooms, interspersing these with generous bunches of the tradescantia, which should break up the density of the petalled blooms and support them at the same time.

ali babar

the mood is exotic,
romantic, bountiful

elements
Very open (fully blown) roses, palm fronds (leaves) and date palm fronds (*Phoenix dactylifera*) (the flowering part of the palm that bears date seeds and fruit). The roses should look as if they are almost 'falling apart'. When buying your roses, choose an eclectic mix of styles, shapes, and hot and warm colours — hot pinks, lemons, oranges, reds, browns — to contrast with the colour of the glazed vase.

Palm and date fronds come in a range of styles and colours of leaves and fruits, depending on the variety. You can purchase date fronds from flower markets, but do look in your own garden — there might be interesting seeds and fronds, both dried and fresh. These can look highly sculptural and are fantastic in a vase, just on their own.

vase type
Use a squat, round vase, cobalt blue or turquoise in colour. A patterned Arabic- or Moroccan-style vessel would also work well. Ideally, any vessel you choose should have a low, wide opening.

method   Arrange the palm leaves in the base of the vase, almost as if you were lining its walls. Make sure that some of the leaves rise up from the sides and show their beautiful shape. In the arrangement pictured opposite, the palm leaves have been trimmed with scissors to look like a 'fan'.

Fill the vase with water or, if it is not watertight, place a water-filled container inside it and hide it with the palm leaves.

Cut the stems of the roses and arrange the blooms haphazardly, unevenly and loosely. If you have enough roses, let them spill over the side of the vessel. Don't feel compelled to balance their colours or styles. You can also add palm seeds to this arrangement, or create a series of complementary arrangements (two suggestions are shown on these pages).

Buy older, open roses (which are also cheaper than those in bud). Get over the notion that flowers must last seven days — part of the beauty of a flower comes in its final stage of expiring, ephemeral loveliness.

This arrangement is most effective when placed on the floor, or on a landing, a verandah or a low bench. The design can be much better appreciated when you are looking down on it.

bacchic

seasonal plenty, rampant fecundity

elements   Ornamental cotoneaster berries and rosella berries (*Hibiscus heterophyllus*). The name of this arrangement may evoke images of grapevines and fruits (and the ensuing ecstasies and atrocities, as the Greek myth goes); however, similarly shaped but longer-lasting mixed berries are the elements here. This arrangement is one of the simplest. Cotoneaster and its red berries are frequently seen growing in gardens, often in hedges. Its lovely foliage will last for weeks in a vase. Rosella berries, also red, look quite rustic and lovely. (Please note that *neither* of these berries is edible.)

vase type   Use a large, rustic glazed pot that can support any size of branch that you wish to incorporate (the bigger the better, as cotoneasters have a rapacious growing habit and produce very large branches in twisted shapes). Use a richly coloured pot — dark green, ochre, umber, dark red — that will complement the red and green of the berries and foliage. Unglazed terracotta is not rich enough to match the tones of the berries and foliage. You could try a patterned vessel, but be careful with the colours and size of the pattern.

method   Fill the vessel with water. If it is not watertight, it might be better to use a plastic container inside the vessel. Strip the cotoneaster branches of any leaves and berries that would be submerged. As you arrange the branches, look at their shape and direction. The rosella berries seem to last well out of water and dry really well too. Lay them in a mound at the base of the pot filled with cotoneaster berries, as a complementary gesture.

You may need to secure the pot so that it doesn't tip over from the weight of the branches. Before you start arranging, partly fill the pot with sand and then insert a plastic container to hold the water, sitting within the pot but above the sand. Of course, this technique would not suit a clear glass vase.

bazaar

a tantalizing array of fruits and fronds

elements
Sugar bananas (*Musa* x *paradisiaca*), tropical leaves (such as *Molineria capitulata*), dried palm fronds and husks. Once they have dried and fallen to the ground, you can collect the palm husks and fronds from gardens. Keep an eye out for palm fronds that have been cut back from trees and put out by the roadside for green waste collection. You can also purchase these fresh at the market. If they are cut green, small clusters of sugar bananas have a very long life. Eventually, of course, they do yellow and ripen.

vase type
Tall, unglazed ceramic or earthenware vessels, or sets of vessels to create a cluster effect, are best. Because the main components of the arrangement are dried, unglazed vessels will complement the dehydrated and rustic materials.

method
There is no need for water in this arrangement, which makes it well suited to placement in hard-to-access areas, such as on top of a tall pillar. Loosely arrange the palm husks and the leaves in the opening of the vessel. You might prefer to start with green leaves and palm fronds and husks, so that they dry *in situ*. Once the dried matter is in place, add the clusters of sugar bananas, resisting the temptation to place them in the foreground, or as the focal point of the arrangement. When the bananas are fully ripe, promptly remove them.

Once you are satisfied with your dried sculptural arrangement, you can easily add fresh highlights, giving the arrangement a seasonal lift from time to time. Secrete a small plastic container, capable of holding water, among the palm fronds and insert the fresh material, or use plastic vials (see page 72).

Experiment with drying
various palm leaves; some
varieties work better
than others, depending on
the shape and colour of
the dried form.

Voluptuous damask roses and weeping
vines of passionfruit in flower, offset
by crab apple branches.

harem

seductive as an odalisque;
brazen and beautiful

elements

Roses (*Rosa gallica*), passionfruit vine (*Passiflora* species), beefsteak plant foliage (*Iresine herbstii* 'Brilliantissima'), crab apple branches (*Malus* species), purple hydrangeas and pomegranate branches (*Punica granatum*). Fuchsia-coloured damask roses with double petals look exaggerated and voluptuous, like the flowers you would expect to find in a harem. Blooming in summer, these roses can be enjoyed for only a few days in the vase. Use masses of roses if you can get them. Ensure that the roses are not fully open when you buy them so that they last for more than one day. In the meantime, the more open roses will start to drop their petals: enjoy the lovely effect.

Passionfruit vine too, once cut, does not have a very long vase life, but if you grow it in your garden, do cut a few trails when it is in flower. It is such an exotic-looking flower. The passionfruit flower and vine both seem to complement the roses well.

Crab apple branches also fruit in late summer, the apples resembling gorgeous little clusters of cherries rather than apples. Incorporate them into this arrangement as a backdrop to this seductive scene of plenty. With or without leaves, crab apple branches also look fantastic on their own. Stripped, these branches have quite an oriental feel, and they look sublime in an oriental-style vase with tall lotus flowers and leaves. And these fruiting branches last a very long time in a vase.

Here pomegranate branches frame an urn filled with damask
roses, beefsteak plant foliage and purple hydrangeas.

vase type

If you can't find crab apple branches or the passionfruit vine,
then you could use darkening purple hydrangeas and pomegranate
branches that are also readily available in summer.

You will need two or three separate vessels to accommodate the
different combinations of flowers and foliage. Coppery silver
pails, used for making yoghurt in Middle Eastern countries, are
perfect for flower arrangements. Look in homeware shops
specializing in Middle Eastern goods. The sheen of the vessels
adds another element. An eclectic mix of stone and earthenware
would also be suitable.

method

Fill the vessels with water. If you are using earthenware
containers that may be unsealed, insert a plastic container
inside the vessels. Carefully strip the rose stems and the
passionfruit vine of the leaves that would be submerged. For this
arrangement, do not strip the crab apple branches of leaves
(except for those that would be submerged, of course), as they
add to the sense of abundance. Arrange the passionfruit vine in
one of the vessels first; you may need to coil it inside the
vessel once or twice in order to anchor it in place. If you
wish, wrap the vine around the base of the vessel but in such a
way that it shows its flowers to best advantage. Add the roses
to this vessel, spreading them out and allowing them to weep over
the sides of the vessel. Finally, create other complementary
arrangements. For example, use the pomegranate branches as either
a background or foreground feature to offset the combination of
hydrangeas and roses.

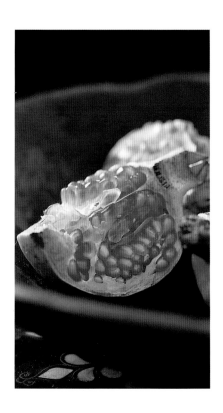

The seeds of the pomegranate are like little
crimson jewels.

salome

feminine and ferocious,
enigmatic and alluring

elements
Black garden roses and asparagus fern (*Asparagus sprengeri*). This arrangement is a good example of how simple combinations of flowers can look modern and devastatingly beautiful at the same time. As they unfurl, black roses have an incredible black velvet sheen on the tips of their deep red petals, which is quite eerie. Use the asparagus fern to veil and wrap the flowers, thereby creating a sense of mystery. The emerald green of the fern is a perfect foil for the black-red of the roses. Look at textures too — black velvet and feathery, lacey-patterned emerald green. But there is more — the filtering of light through the asparagus fern veil. Just gorgeous.

vase type
A low, rounded, voluptuous vessel suits this arrangement: the asparagus fern should billow out around it. Because the floral elements are so simple in this arrangement, you can choose a vessel that is a bit extravagant. Ideally, it should be silver and reflective, with handles or filigree or other decorative elements.

method
Carefully strip the rose and asparagus fern stems of excess foliage that would be submerged. Arrange the fern in the vessel first; to anchor it in place, you may need to coil it inside the vessel one or two times. Try to create the effect of a sumptuous nest for the roses, with the loose and wispy end pieces making a floaty veil around the vessel. Arrange the fern pieces so that they filter light. You could also wrap the vine around the base of the vessel in such a way that the vessel and black roses are shown to best advantage. Add the roses in a clustered group, deep in the centre of the asparagus fern nest.

subaqueous

phosphorescence

coolly restrained and minimal

elements Lotus flowers, or other water lily varieties, and lotus pods (*Nelumbo* species). Other aquatic plants could also create an interesting composition. Generally, large leaves can look very effective when they are magnified under water; they also tend to last longer than submerged flowers.

vase type Use a vase that is rounded, or almost spherical, like a fishbowl. This shape tends to amplify the stems, flowers and foliage that are submerged in the vase.

method Start by almost filling the vase with water. It is easier to arrange the flowers under water, and then gently top up the water, than to add the water at the end and risk disturbing the finished arrangement.

Cut the stems of the flowers and foliage vertically and place each one inside the vase, pushing it gently under the water and into place. The flowers, in particular, are likely to float a little, and you will need to balance them in position by nudging their stems against the glass. It may take a few tries to position them. Once you have more flowers, pods or leaves submerged, it will become easier to keep them all where you want them.

Keep this arrangement simple. If you include lots of flowers and stems, the design under water will become too busy and confusing. Keep it all in proportion to the size and shape of the vessel.

The lotus flowers will only last a day or so under water. However, the leaves and lotus pods will look fine for a number of days.

The water reed stems flex in very interesting ways and will stay sharply bent once you snap them over. Create a sculpture by leaving most of the reeds standing vertically, but selectively bend a few of them. When you have tired of the reeds in the vase, try twisting them into a wreath (see page 77).

(see page 77).

You can buy basic varieties of water reeds from your local plant nursery, but for exotics go to a specialist aquatic plant nursery.

simple beauty distilled to its essence

elements
Water reeds, such as mini bulrush (*Typha* species). You can purchase an amazing variety of aquatic plants from specialist water plant nurseries.

Alternatively, if you live near a river or lake, you might be able to collect wild water reeds that grow rampantly on their banks as well as in shallow water. What appears to be a rather ordinary, weedy plant has amazing potential: both the hollow cylindrical stems of the plant and the brown tangled nest of its root system have wonderful sculptural qualities when displayed beneath glass. Isolating very simple natural forms in a vase can create powerful organic art works.

vase type
Choose a very simple, tall, clear glass vase that can support the height of the reeds. The uncluttered shape and style of the vase complements the simple forms of the arrangement.

method
Depending on the proportions of your vase, use 1-3 water reed plants. Remove all silt from the roots, then pat the roots dry with paper towels to remove any excess residue. If you leave any silty residue on the roots, the water will be muddy and obscure part of the arrangement. You will need to pour a little water onto the root system to keep the plant itself green for a week or two, otherwise the stems will begin to dry out very quickly. Place the plants in the vase and focus on arranging the root systems into an interesting nest at the base of the vase. Using a small jug, gently pour a small amount of water over the roots again, just enough to moisten them and sustain the plant, for a little while at least. Then focus on the reeds themselves, bending a few over to create a sculptural effect.

buoyant

floating world:
water splashed, weightless

elements

Water lily pads (*Nymphaea* species). Some tropical varieties of lily pads have gorgeous patterns and variegated colours, and look like patterned leather. The ones used here even have water splash patterns on them in deep burgundy and greens. Specialist water plant nurseries should offer a range of water lily pads.

vase type

Choose a low, rustic, wooden boat-style vessel that is watertight. It should contrast well with the colours of the lily pads, and it should also draw attention to the water line between the lily pads and the vessel. The lily pads should float on the surface of the water, appearing light and buoyant.

method

Fill the vessel with water, almost to the rim. It might need to be *in situ* first if it is large, as filling a vessel entirely with water increases the weight threefold. Float the lily pads, arranging them so that interesting aspects of the leaves are highlighted. For example, the leaves pictured have a variegated splash pattern on the top, and a deep red on the underside, so lift up some of the pads to create a curve above the water line and display the rich colour underneath. Lily pads in a water-filled vessel can last for months, either indoors or outdoors.

You could submerge these leaves to amplify the gorgeous patterns of their leaves, and float water lily blooms instead.

This arrangement would also look great in a low, round, clear glass vessel so that all parts of the lily pads, especially their interesting stems, could be displayed.

Driftwood and dried palm veil are complemented by
the fractured colours of this distressed table.

driftwood

bleached and bare; cast ashore, abandoned

elements
Driftwood and bleached organic forms. When you visit the sea or a
river, search for interesting pieces of weathered wood that you
can use as organic sculptures in your home. Each bleached and
weathered surface is unique. The tone and texture of driftwood
pairs very well with other bleached organic matter, such as dried
palm veil, pictured in this arrangement, so always look for these
similarities in colour and texture.

The other lovely thing about dried sculptures is that you can mix
dried matter with fresh flowers on special occasions, or whenever
you discover flowers that will suit your evolving sculpture for a
short while. You can use plastic vials filled with water to hold
the flower stems (see page 72).

method
This driftwood sculpture should not be contained in a vessel; its
form is best suited to an outdoor position, such as on a rustic
table on a verandah, or the step of a porch, where it can
metamorphose as you add and subtract elements.

Try mixing fresh flowers or leaves into your evolving sculpture as a welcome
gesture when friends are visiting. And if it is safe to do so, at night
illuminate the weathered crevices with candles held by clam shells (but please
ensure that the driftwood or other dried matter does not catch alight).

nymph

starbursts of saturated colour
    like paper sculptures; simple, slender
party streamers of bamboo

elements   Water lilies (*Nymphaea* species), bamboo foliage and stems. Water lilies are available throughout the summer months in warmer climates and come in a variety of shapes and colours. Buy them fresh from the markets, where they are usually sold as closed buds. Most water lily blooms respond to light and so will close overnight. For a special occasion table setting, these tropical pinks, fuchsias, yellows and purples have an irresistible allure. When mixing bright colours, try to use one kind of flower only and similar coloured tones. Some very simple, thin green or brown bamboo foliage anchors the intensity of the colours. Try not to make the composition too busy.

Water lilies are incredibly resilient. If you find a blemish on a petal, float that water lily in water. It may surprise you with its regenerative properties.

As water lilies are buoyant, you might prefer to float them in an open bowl of water to create your own little pond (see the 'buoyant' arrangement, page 108).

vase type

Teapots not only look cute, they also seem to support individual water lilies very well. This arrangement is more suitable for a table setting, or as a feature on a coffee table or entrance table. Choose vessels that are not too tall and that will enable you to look down upon the open flowers. You can purchase eclectic mixes of Chinese teapots from Asian grocery stores. Choose a selection of heights, diameters and colours. Or look for teapots with a crackle glaze or that lovely celadon sheen; there are so many beautiful oriental-style glazes.

method

Fill the teapots with water, first blocking the spout internally with some plastic wrap or similar, as water does tend to spill out from the spout. Place the bamboo foliage in the teapot opening first, and arrange it so that it anchors the water lilies. Cut the stems of the water lilies vertically and place 2-4 in each teapot. If you are also using thin bamboo stems (not too tall, roughly double the height of the teapots), finish the teapots with these stems, placing them vertically on a little bit of a slant (the way a woman criss-crosses chopsticks through her hair when she ties it up in a bun).

Incorporate some complementary candles into your water lily table setting. Wrap small vases in oriental papers and tie them with some natural twine, bamboo leaf or palm frond. Choose paper that will allow the candlelight to illuminate the design.

Masses of branches in a vase are reminiscent of a densely branched tree.

arboreal

bare branches etched against a pale sky

elements Cork branches (*Quercus suber*) and *Dendrobium* or Singapore orchids. Bare cork branches have a lumpy, woody texture quite unlike any other bark formations. If you are lucky enough to come across these branches at the markets, usually during winter, snatch them up, as they last forever dried and you will never tire of their unique texture.

vase type A warm-coloured vase, such as this one in translucent amber, will suit the warm barky texture of the branches. An elegant stem vase complements the height of the arrangement. As the branches are quite austere, you can use a vase with additional decorative qualities, such as a pattern, or subtle, swirling colours. A translucent vase displays the whole length of the branches, lending an added sense of height and elegance.

method No water is required in the vase. Separate the very tallest branches from the medium and small ones. Arrange the tall branches in the vase first, then add the smaller ones to fill the gaps.

Like the branches in the 'lichen' arrangement, page 122, these cork branches are enhanced by the company of fresh flowers, such as a profusion of orchids in warm colours — yellows, reds, oranges — on long stems. Place the orchid stems into plastic vials of water (see page 72) and secrete the vials between the branches, out of sight. Again, for maximum effect, limit your choice of fresh blooms to one flower type only — en masse — so they don't detract from the austere simplicity of the branches.

When arranging the branches in the vase, shake and brush them first to ensure that they are free of loose fragments and filaments.

lichen

a surreal haze of green on dead boughs, transforming decay into beauty

elements Thin, bare branches covered in lichen and fresh flowers, such as hydrangeas or Asiatic hybrid liliums. In cool climates at a high altitude, bare branches of deciduous trees are often covered in lichen and moss. Lichen in particular can look like eerie and fantastical foliage in place of the natural leaves. The beauty of these branches is that they last forever; the dried lichen does not lose its (almost supernatural) sage green colour. Look for branches in different shapes and sizes, the common element being a covering of lichen. This arrangement uses two very tall privet branches (*Ligustrum* species), placed in isolation in one vase, accompanied by a dense cluster of low-lying, lichen-covered dry branches in the other vase. The combination of dense and sparse elements, using the same organic material and colours, provides immense interest in itself.

For a Christmas tree with a modern twist, hang your lichen-covered branches with silver and glass decorations. They will look particularly stunning against the sage green and grey of the branches, which should be sturdy enough to hold the weight of any festive adornments. However, be sure to weight the vessel containing the branches with sand or pebbles.

vase type   The sage green of the lichen and the grey of the branches go
             extremely well with oriental vases in blues, green, celadon and
             crackled or patterned blue and white glazes. Vases in cool
             colours work best with the mood set by the form and colour of
             the bare branches. A cluster of large vases would be ideal for
             this arrangement, as you should isolate the sparse, tall branches
             from the dense, lower clusters. You can also add fresh flowers to
             a third or even a fourth vase; in that way you won't need to
             disturb the dried composition with water.

method   Arrange the tall sparse branches and the dense cluster of low
             branches in their respective vases.

             The branches also look great in the company of fresh flowers,
             such as a generous bunch of green or white hydrangeas, or even
             white Asiatic hybrid liliums. For maximum effect, limit the
             composition of the fresh flowers to one massed type of flower
             only. This will complement the austere simplicity of the two
             branch compositions. (See the arboreal design, page 118.)

Take care when tranporting the branches home, as the lichen
can be knocked off the branches quite easily.

medusa

cascading jade tentacles

elements
Medusa leaves (*Anthurium vitarifolium*) and cactus stems (*Rhipsalis* species). The green leaves of the medusa are, as its namesake suggests, very serpent-like in appearance. According to Greek mythology, Medusa was a monstrous female creature, with live snakes for hair and a gaze that turned men to stone. Certain creeping cactus plants also grow in a tendril-like fashion, and when they are combined with the sleek and velvety medusa leaves, they make a gothic composition of textured greens that can suit a surprising range of interior styles.

vase type
This arrangement is built around an elegant, gilt, wall-mounted metal vessel with a leaf motif. Many ornate, wall-mounted antique light fittings, corbels and mirrors have features that are ideal for supporting draped foliage. Use your imagination and select foliage that will last for an extended period without water. If you do not have gilt ornaments at your disposal, any type of vase — from very ornate to clear glass — would work well.

method
Simply drape the medusa leaves and cactus stems over and through the ornamental vessel of your choice. If you are using a vase, position the medusa leaves first; they have a lovely flexibility, allowing you to twist them inside the vessel to keep them in place. Their ends should slither out of the vase. Add the cactus as a finishing touch. The weight of these stems will also keep those slithering medusa leaves in check. Both will last out of water for weeks. And take care with the spikes on the cactus, as the finer needles can be difficult, and painful, to remove from your fingers.

The medusa leaves and cactus stems would even look fabulous hanging off a glass chandelier.

The strelitzia beak may contain properly formed but dormant multiple flower crests. Once the primary crest has dulled, cut it off, then reach into the middle of the beak and gently push these young crests up to the surface.

carnivore

primal, tribal, almost predatory

elements
Strelitzias, tree palm stems, woven palm bark and horsetail (*Equisetum* species). Strelitzias (or birds of paradise) have large purple-blue beaks with cream and purple crests. Many palms have wonderful sculptural stems that, once cut and dried, last for months. This arrangement incorporates some stripey cream and green tree palm stems, with textured woven palm bark at their tips, and some interesting stripey horsetail.

vase type
Keep an eye out for old tree stumps with natural crevices, salvagable pieces of wharf piers or monumental pieces of driftwood. Pieces of wood that have been weathered by the elements or submerged under water for some time often have interesting crevices. Insert flowers and leaves in these. If there are no natural cracks or fissures in your stump, you could try cutting your own, or if that's too difficult, cut the stump flat and use it as a plinth. Large pieces of solid wood are difficult to shift around easily, so choose a permanent position near an entrance or on a verandah.

method
If there are no shallow crevices suitable for a plastic container of water, strelitzia flower heads will survive for some time without water. Alternatively, dampen some cotton wool and secure this with string around the base of each strelitzia head. Enclose the damp cotton wool in a clear plastic freezer bag. Arrange the horsetail at the base of the opening; without water, it may dry into interesting shapes. Arrange the horsetail so that it hangs down below the crevice a little. Finish the arrangement by leaning the palm tree sticks against the wooden vessel in a cluster.

herbivore

mouths agape, tender throats
    thrusting out of their leafy nest,
like baby birds waiting to be fed

elements   Sarracenia (or pitcher plant) flowers, mother-in-law's tongue (*Sansevieria trifasciata* 'Laurentii') and variegated rubber tree (*Ficus elastica*) leaves. Sarracenia flowers are gorgeously bizarre things. They have a tube-shaped stem and a flower head in burgundy and green that is designed to trap flies and insects. Their veiny patterns and the frilly lids on the flower heads make these carnivorous plants strangely beautiful. The limey greens of the variegated mother-in-law's tongue leaves combined with the variegated lemon and lime rubber tree leaves emphasize the unique burgundy patterns and unlikely frills on the sarracenia flowers. This arrangement focuses on elongated shapes and a diverse range of patterns, all drawn together by harmonious burgundies and lime greens.

Both the mother-in-law's tongue leaves and the rubber tree leaves last very well out of water for days. In fact, mother-in-law's tongue lasts for months out of water.

vase type   Choose a grey stone garden urn with a stem base that will draw out the shapes of the elongated leaves and sarracenia flowers. The understated, faded colour of the urn makes an interesting contrast with the rich colours of the arrangement. Depending on the mood that you wish to create and the nature of your interior, you shouldn't be afraid to mix rather odd combinations of flowers and vessels. The stone urn pictured — all faded classical elegance — is an unlikely vessel for the starkly modern and sculptural shapes, patterns and colours. But somehow the pairing works. An alternative is to display sarracenia flowers on their own in a clear, tall glass vessel. A single flower in a bud vase can look a little naff, but a sarracenia flower in a tall slim bud vase is rather arresting (if a little phallic).

method   If you are using a stone or cement urn, place a plastic container filled with water inside it, as inevitably the urn will not be watertight. Arrange several mother-in-law's tongue leaves at the back of the arrangement first, adding the variegated rubber tree leaves at the base of the arrangement. The rubber tree leaves might be on tall branches. If they are, position them so that they spill over the urn rim. Classical urns with stems always look gorgeous with branches and vines spilling over the sides. With the rubber tree leaves and branches now *in situ*, there should be enough support for the sarracenia flowers in the foreground of the arrangement.

Rubber tree leaves contain a white rubbery sap that stains surfaces and probably should not go anywhere near your eyes either, so ensure that you rinse freshly cut stems in warm water and dry them off with a paper towel. If you don't do this, the sap will make the water in a vase appear milky.

Sarracenia flowers are expensive due to their relative scarcity as cut blooms, but they do last for more than two weeks in a vase.

equatorial

gingernut

hot, tropical, lush and rich

elements
Torch ginger flowers (*Ettlingera elatior*), anthurium leaves and raffia nuts (*Raphia farinifera*). There are so many beautiful tropical flowers that are enduring, sculptural and exotically gorgeous. Go to the flower markets, or ask your florist to stock the highly sculptural varieties of flowering gingers. Gingers come in a variety of mainly warm colours; they even include flesh- and neutral-toned beehive and 'cigar' varieties. Or you could fill a vase solely with tropical leaves, such as anthurium leaves (like a tortoise shell in pattern and shape, as shown here). Finally, look out for interesting seeds and nuts, such as the raffia nuts pictured.

vase type
Choose a large, preferably squat, wooden vessel, ideally of Indonesian or Javanese teak. The dark wood of the vessel combined with the woody, polished elements of the raffia nuts enhance the vivid greens and warm colours of the flowers.

method
If the vessel is wooden, there is a good chance that it will not be watertight. You might need to insert a plastic container filled with water inside the vase; hide it with the tropical foliage. Fill the vessel with masses of anthurium leaves, followed by the ginger flowers. Cut the blooms quite short so that they are not rising too far above the vessel. Finish the composition by placing the wooden or dried seed components in the arrangement. You can have these elements rising up out of the arrangement so that they are a little higher than the ginger flower.

This arrangement will last at least 1-2 weeks. The gingers may brown a little, depending on the variety. The outer leaves of the hot pink gingers pictured here will eventually shrivel and take on a very Dali-esque appearance when they are finally dried. It's an acquired taste, but some flowers can look spectacular when they are technically dead.

hacienda

from the harshness of the desert,
  the ephemeral delicacy of translucent blooms

elements
Orchid cactus (*Epiphyllum* species). Many varieties of cactus plants flower with spectacular blooms from spring to the end of summer. If you have a flowering cactus plant in your garden, sniff out flowers that might appeal to you before you cut them and take them indoors. Cactus flowers are very similar in blooming habit to water lilies, but in reverse: they open their petals during the evening and close them during the day. So, whether you want open or closed blooms will determine the time of day or night you cut them. In their closed bud state, the flowers — with their subtle greens, browns and flesh tones — resemble overgrown asparagus spikes.

vase type
A low flat vessel or bowl that will allow you to lay out the cactus flowers is best for this arrangement. Given that the flowers can be quite sculptural when in their closed bud state, a glazed or patterned vessel will add additional interest to the composition. Other appropriate choices would be a Mexican-style, glazed ceramic bowl or a low, dark, round wooden bowl.

method
Fill the vessel with enough water to cover the stems of the cactus flowers. Arrange the buds and the more open flowers so the latter are displayed to best effect. You may wish to add some simple green leaves to the arrangement, but the simple repetition of the cactus flower buds seems to work.

Not all varieties of cactus flower have a pleasant perfume, so smell the blooms before you cut them.

This special occasion garland features flowers that will not last more than a day or so. To make the arrangement last a little longer, pluck out any faded blooms and replace them with longer-lasting flowers, such as tiger lilies.

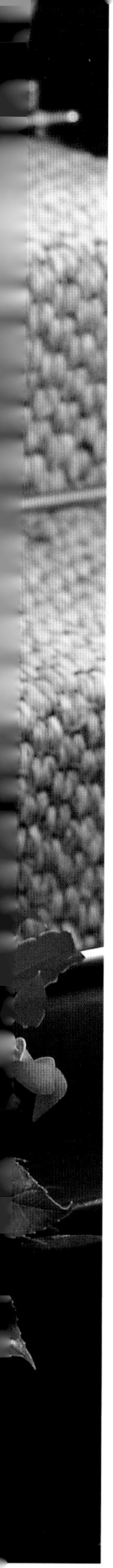

frida

a vivid tropical garland, celebrating the emotion and power of colour

elements

A mix of tropical flowers, such as hibiscus, day lilies (*Hemerocallis* species), calla lilies (*Zantedeschia aethiopica*), tiger lilies (*Lilium lancifolium*), gloriosa lilies (*Gloriosa superba*), passionfruit flowers (*Passiflora* species), frangipani (*Plumeria* species) and oleander (*Nerium oleander*). Choose flowers that are divinely pretty and exotic, but seldom used in flower arrangements due to their tendency to die quickly once cut. Decide on one key colour, such as the reds and dark pinks shown here, and look for flowers in your colour range that have odd little quirks, such as a yellow throat or an orange blush to them, as these will add subtle colour to the composition. Finish with a simple dark green foliage, such as fatsia leaves (which have a lovely hand-like shape).

method

Create the garland structure a few days in advance. This process is a bit tricky, so follow the instructions carefully. The structure is just a sausage shape made from chicken wire, filled with pieces of florist foam.

1 Purchase a roll of fine wire, some fine chicken wire (about 20 cm/8 in wide and up to 1-2 m/3-6 ft long, depending on how ambitious you are feeling), and 2-3 standard bricks of florist foam for every 1 m (3 ft) of chicken wire length. Buy the chicken wire from a hardware store and the foam from a florist supply store.

2 Soak the foam in water until it is saturated (about half an hour).

3 Using a long, sharp knife, cut the foam into thirds.

4 Cut the thirds in half. You should now have 6 pieces of foam.
5 Lay the chicken wire on a level, flat surface outdoors. A slab of concrete is ideal.
6 Begin to shape the chicken wire into a sausage. It is very malleable and will retain its shape. Place the pieces of foam inside the wire sausage, leaving around 5 cm (2 in) at either end. Ensure that there is about 2.5 cm (1 in) between each foam piece to allow for a bit of movement once the chicken wire is closed. You may have to soak and cut more foam if you don't have enough blocks to fill the sausage.
7 Seal the sausage with some fine wire strips. First, bind the two long lengths of the sausage down the middle of the sausage. Then bind the two ends. To make the ends as streamined as possible, scrunch up any excess wire on the ends into the foam. You should now have a fully bound, soggy, foam sausage.
8 Hang the sausage from a clothesline or a tree for a day or two to drain off any excess water.
9 Wear sturdy leather gloves for the next step. Starting at one end of the sausage, scrunch the foam and wire down to about half its original size, moulding it with your hands as you do so. Lots of water should drain from the foam as you do this. The wire casing should keep most of the foam in place, but don't be alarmed if some little bits of foam come out in the process.
10 Once most of the excess water has drained away, leave the sausage to hang and drip excess water for a day or so.
11 The sausage is ready to use when it is dampish to the touch, but not dripping water or leaving watery residue when you place it on a dry surface.

Now, make the pretty garland.

1 Lay the sausage down on a flat surface and distribute the leaves so that they hide a lot of the top surface.
2 Use the larger flowers to disguise any gaps.
3 Finish the composition with smaller blooms, considering the design of the whole garland — the colours, shapes and overall form — as you do so.

Poke each flower or leaf through the chicken wire. Pink frangipanis are ideal for filling in the design.

In addition to producing visually appealing fruit, bananas have large leaves (not shown) that have a beautiful curved shape and texture. For a striking alternative effect, wrap vessels in these large leaves or incorporate them into your arrangements.

strange fruit

ripe with promise, laden with exotic bounty

elements
: Clusters of bananas, young persimmons (*Diospyros* species) and kaffir limes (*Citrus histrix*). You can purchase banana clusters from both flower and fruit markets. The banana cluster itself lasts for weeks out of water, gradually ripening from green to yellow. You can cut young persimmons from the tree while they are still green and enjoy them on their branches in vases while they dry. These young fruits resemble nut pods when they are fully dried. Finally, if you can, buy stems of kaffir lime fruits with their very fragrant leaves still attached.

vase type
: A low, flat, woven basket-like vessel would suit this mix of tropical and fresh ingredients. It will also complement the dried persimmons very well. Or you could try a low, flat, rustic glazed vessel. Either way, a flat vessel best displays the sculptural qualities of the strange fruits.

method
: No water is required for this arrangement, except perhaps to prolong the green freshness of the kaffir lime leaves. You could place the stems in plastic vials before arranging them with the other fruits (see page 72), and then disguise the vials with the banana clusters and persimmons. Arrange the large banana clusters first; to give the arrangement some height, you could try balancing the clusters on top of each other until you achieve the right effect. Curve the kaffir lime branches around the base of the basket, among the banana clusters. It's a nice touch if some branches and fruits spill over the side of the basket too. Finally, add the dried persimmons off to one side to finish the arrangement, letting them spill over.

bamboo

white and green; sun filtered through jungle growth

elements Variegated leaves: alocasia, begonia and *Caladium* species, different varieties of bamboo and dracaena stems, whatever you can find. The bamboos used in this arrangement were picked on a vacant lot. Many bamboo varieties are sold as cut foliage at the flower markets. Look for the straight-stemmed, dark green or variegated varieties, and the new varieties that have twisted and curled stems. Choose 1-3 different varieties of bamboo stems, focusing on different leaf sizes, colours and patterns. You could also add some similar coloured green and patterned tropical leaves, such as anthurium or begonia leaves. The focus in this arrangement is on different shapes and patterns of exotic greens.

vase type Woven bamboo vessels will complement the fresh bamboo. See if you can find vessels woven out of the divine black bamboo variety. A dark ceramic or wooden vessel would work equally well.

method Ensure the vessels are watertight; you may need to secrete a plastic container of water within them. Strip the bamboo stems of foliage and recut them vertically before placing them in water. If you are grouping two or more vessels, use one type of bamboo foliage paired with a selection of green begonia leaves in each: for maximum effect, feature just one variety of bamboo at a time.

The dry black bamboo stem (*Phyllostachys nigra*) used in this woven basket is the perfect foil for the vivid green leaves of *Dracaena sanderiana*.

The beauty of bamboo stems is that they last for weeks in water, and most varieties also sprout roots. If you wish, plant the stems in soil.

azure

succulence

tender softness cradled in woody husks, pink warmth cooled by elements of blue

elements   Small palm husks, blue chalk sticks (*Senecio serpens*), blue hosta leaves and pink peonies. Small palm husks form the base of this table-setting arrangement. Collect them from the base of palm trees. Don't always assume that your flower arrangements need to be contained by a manufactured vessel. As with the 'russet' design, page 34, and the 'bamboo' design, page 148, organic dried materials can be used as natural vessels and may even be more appropriate, adding another dimension to the arrangement. In this design, the palm husk forms a natural boat-shaped vessel for blue chalk stick succulents, loose blue hosta leaves and blown-out pink peony blooms. If peonies are not in season, look for open pink Asiatic hybrid liliums, tiger lilies, large tulips or David Austin roses. The mix of exaggerated pink petals and sculptural blue succulents is particularly striking. The woody palm husks provide an additional focal point for the soft and hard edges, and the tips of the palm husks also emulate the stick shapes of the succulents.

You could enjoy these elements a little longer by rearranging the flowers, succulents and hosta leaves in a low bowl of water.

vase type   The palm husks are the natural vessels in this arrangement.

method   Lay the palm husks down the centre of your dinner table, or in a
central cluster if your table is circular. Lay the blue chalk
stick succulents in clusters among the palm husks. Once home to
baby palm seeds, each husk has a natural boat shape, so use this
hollow to balance the succulents. In fact, you should be able to
stand the succulents vertically if you wish, as the 'sticks' have
a natural curve to their stem. Position the softer spade shapes
of the blue hosta leaves among the succulents. Finish the
arrangement by placing single peonies in plastic vials filled
with water (see page 72) before positioning them in the crevices
of the palm husks, among the succulents and leaves. Take care to
conceal the plastic vials. The peonies should be positioned to
show off their intricate stamens.

If you have some hosta leaves left over, tie one around each
table napkin. Another idea is to tie a small tag to each leaf
and use it as a place card.

Each palm husk is a boat-shaped vessel, perfect
for holding the blue chalk sticks in place.

Use any leftover hosta leaves as
plate decorations.

You will need to place
each peony stem in a
small plastic vial
filled with water
(see page 72).

prickly pear

graphic, modern, serenely eccentric

elements

Blue chalk sticks (*Senecio serpens*) and prickly pear cactus branches (*Opuntia* species). A great many succulent and cacti varieties are a lovely, dusty, blue-grey shade. They can look quite surreal and beautiful, as well as very modern. Succulents are often arranged in a manner that can be quite severe, but if you arrange an interesting composition of forms, the delicacy of the succulent stems visually balances the hard and prickly edges of the cactus.

vase type

A vintage battery acid vase is worth its weight in gold if you can find one; have a look around in antique shops. This vase is made from pale blue glass rather than the standard green or clear variety. Alternatively, choose a glass vase in translucent pale blue, or one in clear glass, with a bit of height, that will display the prickly pear branches to their full advantage.

method

Wear thick garden gloves to handle the prickly pear, as the spikes are treacherous. Remove the thorns by brushing down the sides of each branch with your glove. Don't disturb the dusty film that covers many blue succulents and cacti: you'll leave fingerprints.

Place two branches in the vessel, and try to create interesting shapes and lines both below and above the water line. Next, add the bunches of succulents, still secured with a plastic band (if this adds to the composition, bearing in mind the vase used). Look at the direction and placement of the prickly pear and position the succulents in relation to these. Soften this arrangement further by adding simple, structural flower forms, such as chincherinchee (*Ornithogalum thyrsoides*, asparagus-like spears with many heads of white flowers) or hyacinths.

This arrangement is long lasting. You will find that most succulents will sprout roots in water, so plant the blue chalk stick succulents in a pot when you have finished with the arrangement.

spike

perched, ready to creep away
                on fleshy, serrated blue limbs

elements   Aloe vera and orchid roots. The spines on aloe vera look cactusy,
but they are really faux spines and not likely to prick you at
all. Many people are surprised to see this sculptural plant
incorporated into floral arrangements, probably because it grows
so readily in their gardens. Aloe vera also lasts very well out
of water for long periods of time. Creepy-looking orchid roots
can be wonderful as a finishing touch, especially when combined
with potted orchids. You can buy these roots in clusters from the
flower markets, or try approaching an orchid grower, who might be
willing to give them to you.

vase type   Salvaged and disused pieces of wharf piers, monumental pieces of
driftwood or tree stumps with natural crevices will house aloe
vera and orchid roots very well. Or use a clear low vase to
reveal all aspects of a tumbled mess of orchid roots and aloe
vera spikes.

If you moisten the orchid roots, the fresher ones will retain a
green colour before gradually drying to bleached tendrils.

This arrangement is mounted on a section of old wharf pier, but a piece of driftwood would also be suitable.

Tiny beads of moisture on the aloe vera stems reflect the light.

method   There is no need for water as the roots and the aloe vera will last for weeks without it; however, if you can hide a plastic container by covering it with roots, you could put the aloe vera stems in water to sustain them. Place clusters of the orchid roots in the crevices of the driftwood or piers, or if you're using a glass vessel, place them at its base. Tidy up the stems of the aloe vera, cutting off older dried leaves if necessary (they peel off the stem very easily). Place the stems in the woody crevices, or in the vase, so that they emerge from the nest of orchid roots.

silvertail

suspend all disbelief: pastel blue
and silver were made for each other

elements Argentum (*Leucadendron argenteum*) leaves and white calla lilies (*Zantedeschia aethiopica*). Argentum leaves are quite surreal, with a soft velvety texture — a shock of cool, sharp silver, the colour of mercury. Argentum foliage must have been created to adorn pastel and white blooms, as if it were a sexy silver mink. The white calla lilies will be transformed into powder blue blooms with floral paint, available from floral supply shops.

vase type Clear glass vases seem perfect for argentum leaves, as are mirrored and glass surfaces. For this arrangement, try using clusters of glass vases of different sizes but of the same shape and style.

method First, spray the calla lilies. Take an individual calla lily and protect the outside of the flower by holding a piece of paper up to the lip of the flower as you lightly spray the inside (try to spray from quite a distance). The sprayed lilies shouldn't take more than a few minutes to dry. Fill the vessels with water and cut the lily stems vertically, then position them in a smaller vase. Strip the argentum stems of those leaves that would be submerged and arrange them in a larger vase, alongside the calla lilies. Some of the argentum branches might be straight up and down, while others (younger branches in particular) might have a little more curve and shape to them, so position them according to how you would like the shapes to be seen.

When selecting colours for painting the white calla lilies, avoid darker colours. Hot pink is the darkest you should go. Avoid primary colours too, as the colour sprayed on a white flower will begin to look horribly artificial.

The curly blue leaves of the carnation
stems have a sculptural quality.

blue carnation

frilly and flouncey as a blue tutu

elements Double white carnations (*Dianthus* species) and hosta leaves.
Double carnations can easily be mistaken for peonies and,
certainly, they have a longer season than peonies and don't blow
open and die in a day. In fact carnations can last beyond two
weeks in a vase, and they also have a nice smell. Carnations are
a member of the succulent family: you only have to take a closer
look at the stem (see the detail above) to see sculptural, curly
blue leaves. It is elementary that carnations (especially in
pastel lemon, pink, orange and even blue) would look great with
sharp blue succulents, such as blue chalk sticks (*Senecio
serpens*) or aloe vera (akin to the sharp and soft textures of
the 'succulence' design, page 154).

vase type Choose a kooky, pale blue glass vase in an interesting shape,
with a pattern or embossed design. That coloured 1960s glass with
'Barbarella' curves would be perfect.

method To spray paint the carnations, follow the method outlined in the
'silvertail' design, page 166. Then fill the vase with water, and
cut the stems of the hosta leaves before positioning them around
the mouth of the vase. Add the carnations above the foliage. The
lovely spade shape of the hosta leaves should frame the mass of
carnations in a cute way, like a Peter Pan collar.

Hosta leaves have a limited season during summer, so if they are not available, try using some blue
succulents, such as spiky agave fronds or the blue chalk sticks used in the 'succulence' design, page 154.

verdant

bud

fresh and joyous and new —
bring spring indoors

elements
Any branches with spring buds. Just go into your garden at the onset of spring and clip branches bursting with buds of flowers or foliage. You should be able to buy branches of fruit blossoms from the markets and florists, but try to be adventurous with other plants that have interesting leaf formations.

vase type
The vessel should be of very simple, or otherwise highly decorative, glass. As the arrangement is so plain, coloured glass is also a lovely option. Glass is best as it doesn't detract from the form of the new leaves or flowers that are emerging from the bud. Two vintage 'tear drop' green glass shades have been used in the design shown here. Hang them together from a doorway, or on a verandah or windowsill.

method
Clip 2-4 small branches from the chosen tree (ash, *Fraxinus* species, has been used here). Fill the vessel with water and immerse the branches immediately. Arrange the forms in whatever way takes your fancy. The focus of the design should be on interesting woody stem shapes and unfurling buds.

There is no need to batter wooden stems before immersing them in water in order to extend their vase life. The best treatment for branches and stems is to harvest them by making a clean cut with sharp secateurs. Recutting the stems and changing the water frequently will also help. This arrangement should last at least 2-3 weeks if you look after it.

The stems of these alocasia leaves have been
deliberately curved into the vase.

To change the look, you could add one kind
of fresh, spear-like flower, such as white chincherinchee
(*Ornithogalum thyrsoides*) or even white gladioli spikes.

evergreen

photosynthesis in a vase

elements Alocasia leaves. With their gorgeous spade-shaped leaves, long
elegant stems and vivid green colour, these leaves can sustain an
arrangement on their own. They are so fresh looking: you can tell
that these leaves grow and thrive in shady places. Rarely do
medium-sized leaves possess such lovely long stems, making it
possible to enjoy them in a tall vase, as you would a bunch of
tall-stemmed blooms. This arrangement of leaves illustrates the
role stems play as an integral part of the overall composition.

vase type If you can find one, a tall, green, translucent vase is ideal.
Otherwise, choose a clear, tall vase or other translucent glass
vessel — anything that will accentuate the stems of the leaves
within the confines of the vase itself.

method Fill the vase to about a quarter full with water. Why? The end of
the stems will be curved and amplified under the water line,
while the stems between the water line and the lip of the vase,
where the leaves will rest, will be above the water line. Cut the
stems vertically. When placing the ends of the stems in the vase,
push them into one corner to create a slight curve, and rest the
leaves on the lip of the vase to support the curve formation.
Finish the arrangement so that the leaves are spilling over the
lip of the vase.

deciduous

mellowing into muted beauty

elements

Belladonna lilies (*Amaryllis belladonna*), lotus leaves (*Nelumbo* species) and browning hydrangea blooms. As summer fades into autumn, capture the seasonal transition in the life of flowers and leaves in your floral compositions. Hydrangea is a readily available flower that captures this transition well. Although it is associated with cottage gardens, its tiny florets can be quite sophisticated in the way they balance the conventionally pretty and the sculptural. By the beginning of autumn, its vivid blues, purples and greens have begun to fade to muted olives, reds, browns and purples.

The belladonna lily grows from a bulb and blooms at the end of summer, in clusters of fragrant white and pink bell-shaped flowers. When this lily finishes blooming, it leaves an equally amazing legacy — the belladonna pod. It is a spike with multiple prongs, each ending with a round cluster of flower seeds, encased by a fine membrane. The colour of this seed membrane is fantastic too — vivid green mellowing to brown and salmon.

In warmer climates, lotus leaves are available in summer; in the tropics they last for longer periods. The lotus flower, pods and leaf return to dormancy beneath the water line in winter. Cut lotus leaves carry a delicious, heavy green smell. Like other aquatic plant leaves, the lotus leaf has a round shape with wonderful veins that run to the centre of the leaf stem. It is a bluey grey-green, with lighter green patterns in the centre of the leaf that resemble a dark water stain. Once cut, the water-filled leaves begin to 'rigor mortise' immediately. The leaves assume fantastical shapes that resemble blown-out parachutes, or the swirl of a dancer's skirt. You can enjoy the leaves during this transition and once they are fully dried in their final postures.

Belladonna pods look amazing when arranged with other mellowing flowers and leaves. For a fresher look, team the pods with branches of autumn leaves and white Asiatic hybrid liliums or November lilies (*Lilium longiflorum*).

If you are able to find a grower who will sell you the lotus leaves, ensure that they are freshly cut on the day that you intend to use them. Enjoy cutting their stems, which give off a stretchy fibrous residue.

vase type   Any clear vase would look good with this arrangement. If possible, retain the length of the stems. The long neck of the vase pictured on page 177 elongates the whole arrangement and draws attention to the patterns formed by the stems, in an otherwise quite top-heavy composition. So look for an elegant vase with an interesting stem and neck. Given the subtlety of colours in the metamorphosing flowers, leaves and pods, avoid coloured glass and patterned vessels. A transparent green glass vase would overwhelm the subtle colours of the arrangement.

method   Fill the vase with water and arrange the belladonna stems off to one side. Consider the criss-cross of the belladonna stems, as they will be amplified under the water and thus form an important part of the composition too. Before arranging the hydrangeas, drench the flower heads in water, then shake them off. Remember that hydrangea flowers and leaves are incredibly porous and love to drink up water through their stems, leaves and flowers. Once they are *in situ*, mist the flowers and leaves with a spray each day. Cut the stems of the hydrangeas vertically, and add long-stemmed clusters in the opposite direction to the belladonna pods, again looking at the criss-cross effect of the stems underwater as you do so. Finally, if the composition is to be placed in such a way that it has a 'front', add 3-4 lotus stems at the back of the arrangement; otherwise, keep them in a cluster separate to the hydrangea flowers and the belladonna pods. Don't mix up the elements in a bitsy fashion: clusters of shapes and forms maximize the impact of the arrangement.

The bluey green of the lotus leaves looks amazing with pink flowers. Try this fantastic composition: bluish-tinged palm fronds (butia palm, *Butia capitata*), calla lilies (*Zantedeschia aethiopica*) sprayed a pale pink colour and dried lotus leaves.

sage

take risks with proportion and tone —
          combine unassuming loveliness
with classical refinement

elements
: Lambs' tongue leaves (*Stachys byzantina*). Of all the leaves, lovely, downy lambs' tongue leaves are the nicest to touch. Wouldn't you just love to lie in a bed of them?

vase type
: The twist in this arrangement is that rather than use small clusters of leaves in a low vase, as you would normally expect, try to make something monumental and even quite formal out of the clusters of leaves by arranging them in a tall, striking stem vase. Use a clear vase to accentuate the repetitive pattern of the crammed-in stems beneath the water line.

If you can, position this simple but elegant arrangement in front of a mirror in a light-filled room.

Lambs' tongue leaves have a woolly texture that invites you to
not only touch them, but also rub your cheek against them!

method   Try to buy lambs' tongue leaves that are crisp and not too
          saggy, on stems as long as possible and not too brown on the
          tips. You may wish to trim the stems of any brown bits, or else
          see how they look in the vase: in a very simple composition, the
          browning of the stems may well add an attractive element.
          However, if the stems are a little slimy, the water will become
          cloudy and deteriorate.

          Cut the stems of the leaves, but try not to cut them too
          perfectly. The overall simplicity of this arrangement is enhanced
          by odd little quirks such as uneven stems. Arrange the leaves so
          that they spill over the the lip of the vessel and thus soften
          that harsh line. The downy leaves, the odd little uneven stems
          and the band of clean water beneath them are all equal partners
          in this austere composition. This arrangement becomes more
          appealing if it is amplified and reflected by a mirror in a
          light-filled position.

olio

memories of archaic olive groves;
fundamental, iconic, unadorned

elements Olive branches (*Olea europaea*). The leaves of the olive tree have a beautiful colour — a mix of grey-green leaves with a silver back, the silver becoming more predominant as the branches dry. The simple elegance of the branches and the sublime colour of the foliage are best enjoyed on their own, without too many other elements to distract the eye.

vase type Because the branches are so simple and elegant, a very simple, clear glass vase, perhaps in an interesting shape, would suit this composition. If you are lucky enough to find a battery acid vase, snap it up, as it is a good design investment piece. The glass used in battery acid vases is generally thicker so you are less likely to chip and break these resilient pieces.

method Fill the vase with water and trim off any olive leaves that would be submerged in water. Cut the stem of each branch vertically before placing it in water. Some floristry technique books recommend battering woody stems with a hammer or similar weapon, but you can avoid such brutality: just leave the branch to draw up the water through the clean cut in the stem. To extend the vase life of your arrangement, change the water and recut the stems as often as possible.

If you become tired of the simplicity of the silvery leaves and branches, freshen the arrangement with some white flowers, such as white Asiatic hybrid liliums or November lilies (*Lilium longiflorum*).

index

raffia (*Raphia farinifera*), nuts, 136-7
ranunculus, 16
Raphia farinifera, 136-7
'reed' design, 106-7
Rhipsalis sp., 126-7
'rooted' design, 72-3
rosehips, 34-7, 76
rosella berries (*Hibiscus heterophyllus*), 86-9
roses
   black, 98-9
   damask, 94-7
   David Austin, 20, 24, 78, 155
   fully blown, 82-5
   'Julia's Rose', 24-7
rubber tree (*Ficus elastica*), variegated leaves, 130-3
rubia pods, 32-3
'ruby' design, 54-5
'russet' design, 34-7

'sage' design, 182-5
'salome' design, 98-9
Sansevieria trifasciata 'Laurentii', 130-3
sarracenia flowers, 130-3
saviour grass (*Dasypogon bromeliifolius*), 44-7
Schefflera actinophylla, 54-5
sedge (*Carex* 'Frosted Curls'), 44-7
seed pods, 38, 42-3
senecio, 22-3
Senecio serpens, 154-9, 160-1, 168
silver acacia, 76
'silvertail' design, 166-7
Singapore orchids, 118-21
smoke bush (*Cotinus coggygria*), foliage, 56-7
snowberries (*Symphoricarpus* sp.), 24
sorghum grass, 44-5
Spanish moss (*Tillandsia usneoides*), foliage,
   72
'spike' design, 162-5
split compositions, 54, 67, 68, 70-1, 96-7
spray painting, 166, 181
Stachys byzantina, 182-5
stem vases, 51
stephanotis, 50-3
sticks
   dried, 68-71
   dyed black, 68
   ginger stems, 38-41
'stix' design, 38-41
'strange fruit' design, 146-7
strelitzias, 128-9
'succulence' design, 154-9
succulents, 161, 168
blue, 168
sugar bananas (*Musa x paradisiaca*), 90-1

sunflowers (*Helianthus* sp.)
   seed heads, 32-3
   seeds, 32
Symphoricarpus sp., 24

table settings
   candles with water lilies, 114-15
   float bowl, 28
   'russet' design, 34-7
   'succulence', 154-9
tetra nuts (*Eucalyptus tetrodonta*), 76
textures, 10, 43
tiger lilies (*Lilium lancifolium*), 78, 142-5, 155
Tillandsia usneoides, 72
torch ginger (*Ettlingera elatior*), flowers, 136-7
Tradescantia pallida 'Purple Heart', 78-9
tree palm stems, 128-9
tree stumps, 129, 162
tulips, 155
   Parrot tulips, 78
Typha sp., 106-7

umbrella tree (*Schefflera actinophylla*), red spikes,
   54-5

'vanille' design, 22-3
'vanity fair' design, 16-19
vases, 13
   battery acid vase, 161, 186
   clusters of, 54, 67, 68, 70-1, 96-7
   stem vase, 51
   tear drop glass shades, 172-3
   see also containers
vessels *see* containers; vases
vials, plastic, for water, 50, 52, 72
vine, gnarled, 74

water, 13
   keeping clean, 19, 22, 32
water lilies (*Nymphaea* sp.), 102-3, 112-15
   pads, 108-9
water reeds, 106-7
'winsome' design, 24-7
wire, 13
wisteria vines, 74, 77
woody stems, 19, 173
wreaths, 74-7

yucca flower spikes, 68-71

Zantedeschia aethiopica, 142-5, 166-7, 181
zebra grass (*Miscanthus sinensis* 'Zebrinus'), 44-7
Zingiber sp., 38-41, 137

acknowledgments

Thanks to Alan B and Sarah D for their collaboration on this book (Alan, thanks for your tireless persistence in getting *the* shot — we do love it). Thanks to Marylouise, but more so to Freddy, for jumping up on my white jeans with his muddy paws that fateful day (totally my fault for wearing white jeans at a dog park). Thank you to Kay for taking this chance, and also to Diana (you poor thing, please stop me from being way too verbose).

Thanks to the following wonderful people who permitted me to use their beautiful homes, stores and *objets d'art* as a real context for these designs: Hainy and Mary Teague; Irene and David; Shannon and Michael; Marea at A Turkish Bazaar; Rob, Ali and Julia at Manning & Manning; and Karin, Michael and Alison at Ruby Star Traders.

Special special thanks to my dear friend Rosemary and her partner Russell for gliding into my store with Tildy, who inspired me with her wonderful jewellery and her use of the term 'chichi', then allowed me to use her home on several occasions, being so gracious when I sprayed a mouthful of champagne over our riverdancing photographer Alan in her kitchen. (I remain horrified to this day.)

Thanks also to Gowan and Grant; Lawrence and Anna; Rick E, Steve and Jose for growing such beautiful things (or otherwise sourcing them, in the first instance), for your loyalty (so rare these days) and for some market insights along the way.

Finally, I'd like to acknowledge the following artworks and artists that also feature in this book.

Andreas Reiter Raabe, *O.T.*, 2000, acrylic on canvas, private collection, featured in the 'stix' design on page 35.

Panchali Sheth, section from *Reflection*, a diptych, featured in the 'ruby' design on page 51.